Preface
Message to the Reader

Rebuilding the Greatest Library in Human History

Thousands of years ago, the Library of Alexandria was the heart of global knowledge — a sanctuary where the wisdom of every known civilization was gathered and shared freely.

And then, it was lost.

Now, we're rebuilding it — and you are invited to join us.

At the Library of Alexandria, we've set out to make every book available to every person on Earth — not just in print, but in every language, every format, and for every reader.

Here's how we do it:

- **Deluxe Print Editions at True Printing Cost** - Order any book as a high-quality paperback, elegant hardcover, or stunning boxset — and only pay what it costs to print. No markups. No middlemen.
- **Unlimited Access to the Greatest Works** - Enjoy thousands of timeless classics — from Plato to Shakespeare to Tolstoy — in beautiful, modern eBook and audiobook editions. Read and listen without limits — for every reader, everywhere.
- **Modern Translations for Every Language & Dialect** - We're reimagining the classics in clear, accessible language — and translating them into every dialect imaginable. Everyone deserves to understand humanity's greatest ideas.

When you visit **LibraryofAlexandria.com**, you're not just accessing books — you're joining a global movement to restore, preserve, and share the wisdom of civilization.

Join us today at LibraryofAlexandria.com

Together, we'll ensure the light of human wisdom never fades again.

With gratitude,

The Modern Library of Alexandria Team

Visit:
www.libraryofalexandria.com
Or scan the code below:

The Unparalleled Adventures of One Hans Pfaal

Based on recent reports from Rotterdam, that city appears to be experiencing intense philosophical excitement. Indeed, events have taken place there that are so completely unexpected—so entirely unprecedented—so utterly contrary to established beliefs—that I have no doubt that by now all of Europe is in chaos, all of physics is in turmoil, and reason and astronomy are at complete odds with each other.

It seems that on the—— day of—— (I'm not certain about the exact date), an enormous crowd of people had gathered in the great Exchange square in the well-maintained city of Rotterdam for reasons that weren't clearly specified. The weather was warm—unusually warm for that time of year—with barely a breeze stirring; and the crowd didn't mind being occasionally sprinkled by brief, friendly showers that fell from large white clouds that moved across the blue sky in an unpredictable pattern. However, around noon, a subtle but noticeable disturbance became visible in the gathering: the chattering of ten thousand voices followed; and immediately after, ten thousand faces turned upward toward the sky, ten thousand pipes dropped at the same time from the corners of ten thousand mouths, and a roar that could only be compared to the thundering of Niagara echoed long, loud, and intensely throughout all the surrounding areas of Rotterdam.

The source of this commotion quickly became clear enough. From behind the massive bulk of one of those sharply-outlined cloud formations already described,

The Unparalleled Adventure of One Hans Pfaall

A Whimsical Lunar Voyage—Early Science Fiction, Satire & Bold Imagination

A Modern Translation
Adapted for the Contemporary Reader

Edgar Allan Poe

Translated by Tim Zengerink

Table of Contents

something began to slowly emerge into an open patch of blue sky—a strange, mixed-up, but apparently solid object, so bizarrely shaped and so peculiarly assembled that it couldn't be understood in any way, and could never be properly appreciated, by the crowd of sturdy townspeople who stood gaping below. What could it possibly be? In the name of all the wives and devils in Rotterdam, what could it possibly mean? Nobody knew, nobody could guess; nobody—not even the mayor Mynheer Superbus Von Underduk—had the smallest clue to solve this mystery; so, since nothing more sensible could be done, every single man carefully placed his pipe back in the corner of his mouth, and tilting his right eye up toward the strange sight, puffed, paused, shuffled around, and grunted meaningfully—then shuffled back, grunted, paused, and finally—puffed once more.

In the meantime, however, descending lower and still lower toward the beautiful city, came the object of so much curiosity, and the cause of so much commotion. Within just a few minutes it arrived close enough to be clearly seen. It appeared to be—yes! it was certainly a type of balloon; but surely no such balloon had ever been witnessed in Rotterdam before. For who, I ask, ever heard of a balloon made entirely of dirty newspapers? No person in Holland certainly; yet here, right under the very noses of the people, or rather at some distance above their noses was the exact thing in question, and constructed, I have it on the best authority, of the precise material which no one had ever before known to be used for such a purpose. It was an outrageous insult to the good sense of the citizens of Rotterdam. As for the shape of the phenomenon, it was even more objectionable. Being little or nothing better than a huge sheet of paper turned upside down. And this

3

resemblance was considered by no means diminished when, upon closer inspection, there was noticed a large tassel hanging from its peak, and, around the upper rim or base of the cone, a circle of small instruments, resembling sheep-bells, which kept up a continuous tinkling to the tune of Betty Martin. But still worse. Suspended by blue ribbons to the end of this fantastic machine, there hung, serving as a basket, an enormous gray beaver hat, with a brim extremely broad, and a dome-shaped crown with a black band and a silver buckle. It is, however, somewhat remarkable that many citizens of Rotterdam swore to having seen the same hat repeatedly before; and indeed the whole crowd seemed to regard it with eyes of recognition; while the woman Grettel Pfaall, upon sight of it, uttered an exclamation of joyful surprise, and declared it to be the very hat of her good husband himself. Now this was a circumstance all the more to be noted, as Pfaall, with three companions, had actually disappeared from Rotterdam about five years before, in a very sudden and unexplainable manner, and up to the date of this narrative all attempts had failed of obtaining any information concerning them whatsoever. To be sure, some bones which were thought to be human, mixed up with a quantity of strange-looking debris, had been recently discovered in a secluded location to the east of Rotterdam, and some people went so far as to imagine that in this spot a terrible murder had been committed, and that the victims were in all probability Hans Pfaall and his associates. But to return.

The balloon (for that's certainly what it was) had now dropped to within a hundred feet of the ground, giving the crowd below a clear enough view of whoever was riding in it. This was truly a very amusing little person. He couldn't have been more than two feet tall; but even this small height would have been enough to throw off his balance and tip him over the edge of his tiny basket, if not for a circular barrier that reached up to his chest and was attached to the balloon's ropes. The little man's body was unusually broad for his size, making his whole appearance comically round. His feet, naturally, couldn't be seen at all, though something that looked like a horn-like material occasionally poked through a tear in the bottom of the basket, or more accurately, in the top of what appeared to be a hat. His hands were incredibly large. His hair was very gray and pulled back into a ponytail. His nose was remarkably long, crooked, and red; his eyes were large, bright, and sharp; his chin and cheeks, though lined with age, were wide, puffy, and had a double appearance; but there wasn't the slightest trace of ears anywhere on his head. This strange little gentleman wore a loose overcoat made of sky-blue satin, with matching tight pants that were fastened with silver buckles at the knees. His vest was made of some bright yellow fabric; a white silk cap sat at a jaunty angle on one side of his head; and to finish off his outfit, a blood-red silk handkerchief wrapped around his throat and hung down gracefully on his chest, tied in an elaborate bow of extraordinary size.

Having descended, as I mentioned earlier, to roughly one hundred feet above the ground, the small elderly gentleman was suddenly overcome with nervousness and seemed reluctant to get any closer to the earth's surface. Therefore, he threw out a large amount of sand from a canvas bag, which he lifted with considerable effort, and immediately came to a stop in mid-air. He then began, in a rushed and anxious way, to pull from a side pocket of his overcoat a large leather wallet. He held this suspiciously in his hand, then looked at it with an expression of complete surprise, and was clearly amazed by how heavy it was. He finally opened it, and taking out from it an enormous letter sealed with red wax and carefully tied with red ribbon, dropped it exactly at the feet of the mayor, Superbus Von Underduk. His Excellency bent down to pick it up. But the balloonist, still very upset, and apparently having no other reason to stay in Rotterdam, started at that moment to make hurried preparations to leave; and since it was necessary to drop some ballast to help him rise again, the half dozen bags that he threw out, one after the other, without bothering to empty what was inside them, fell, every single one, most unluckily onto the back of the mayor, and rolled him over and over no fewer than twenty-one times, in front of every person in Rotterdam. It should not be assumed, however, that the great Underduk allowed this rudeness from the little old man to go unpunished. It is reported, on the contrary, that during each and every one of his twenty-one rolls he let out no fewer than twenty-one separate and angry puffs from his pipe, which he gripped tightly the entire time with all his strength, and which he plans to keep gripping until the day he dies.

In the meantime the balloon rose like a lark, soaring high above the city until it eventually drifted quietly behind a cloud similar to the one from which it had so strangely emerged, disappearing forever from the amazed eyes of Rotterdam's citizens. Everyone's attention now turned to the letter, whose descent and resulting consequences had so disastrously undermined both the physical well-being and personal dignity of his Excellency, the distinguished Burgomaster Mynheer Superbus Von Underduk. That official, however, had managed during his spinning movements to spare a thought for the crucial matter of securing the packet in question, which upon examination was found to have fallen into exactly the right hands, being actually addressed to himself and Professor Rub-a-dub in their official roles as President and Vice-President of the Rotterdam College of Astronomy. The letter was therefore opened immediately by these dignitaries on the spot, and was found to contain the following remarkable, and indeed very serious, communication:

"To their Excellencies Von Underduk and Rub-a-dub, President and Vice-President of the States' College of Astronomers, in the city of Rotterdam."

Your Excellencies might remember a humble craftsman named Hans Pfaall, who worked as a bellows repairman and who, along with three others, vanished from Rotterdam about five years ago in a way that everyone must have found both sudden and completely mysterious. However, if it pleases your Excellencies, I, the person writing this letter, am that very same Hans Pfaall. Most of my fellow citizens know well that for forty years I lived and worked in the small square brick building at the end of the alley called Sauerkraut, where I was still residing when I disappeared. My ancestors had also lived there for as long as anyone could remember— they, like myself, consistently practiced the respectable and quite profitable trade of bellows repair. To tell the truth, until recent years when everyone's minds became obsessed with politics, no honest citizen of Rotterdam could want or deserve a better business than mine. Credit was reliable, work was always available, and everywhere there was plenty of both money and goodwill. But as I was explaining, we soon started feeling the impact of liberty and lengthy speeches, and radicalism, and all such things. People who had previously been the finest customers in the world suddenly had no time to think about us at all. They claimed they had all they could handle just reading about the revolutions and keeping pace with the advancement of knowledge and the spirit of the times. If a fire needed fanning, it could easily be fanned with a newspaper, and as the government grew weaker, I'm certain that leather and iron became proportionally more durable, because very quickly there wasn't a single pair of bellows in all of Rotterdam that ever needed a repair or required help from a hammer. This situation could not be tolerated. I quickly became as poor as a church mouse, and having a wife and children to support, my troubles eventually became unbearable, and I spent countless hours thinking about the most practical way to end my life. Debt collectors, meanwhile, gave me little time for such thoughts. My house was constantly surrounded from dawn to dusk, so I began to rant and rage and fume like a caged tiger against the bars of its prison. There were three men in particular who tormented me beyond what I could stand, continuously watching my door and threatening me with legal action. Against these three I secretly swore the most bitter revenge, if I should ever be fortunate enough to get them in my power; and I believe nothing in the world except the pleasure of this expectation kept me from immediately carrying out my suicide plan by shooting myself in the head with a musket. I decided it was better, though, to hide my anger and treat them with promises and kind words until, through some stroke of luck, a chance for revenge might present itself.

One day, after avoiding my creditors and feeling particularly depressed, I wandered aimlessly through the most hidden streets for a long time, until I accidentally bumped into the corner of a bookseller's stall. Noticing a chair nearby for customers to use, I stubbornly threw myself into it and, barely understanding why, opened the pages of the first book that came within reach. It turned out to be a small pamphlet about Speculative Astronomy, written by either Professor Encke of Berlin or a Frenchman with a similar name. I had some basic knowledge about these topics, and quickly became increasingly absorbed in the book's contents, actually reading through it twice before I became aware of what was happening around me. By then it was getting dark, and I headed home. But the treatise had left a permanent mark on my mind, and as I strolled through the dim streets, I carefully went over the author's wild and sometimes incomprehensible arguments in my memory. Certain passages had affected my imagination in a powerful and extraordinary way. The more I thought about these sections, the more intense became the interest that had been awakened in me. My limited education in general, and especially my lack of knowledge about natural philosophy, far from making me doubt my ability to understand what I had read, or causing me to question the many unclear ideas that had emerged as a result, simply served as additional fuel for my imagination; and I was conceited enough, or perhaps sensible enough, to wonder whether those rough ideas which arise in undisciplined minds and have every appearance of truth, might not often actually possess all the strength, reality, and other essential qualities of instinct or intuition; whether, taking this thought one step further, deep thinking itself might not, in purely theoretical matters, be identified as a legitimate source of falsehood and error. In other words, I believed, and still believe, that truth is often by its very nature simple, and that in many cases, the complexity lies more in the depths where we search for her than in the actual places where she can be found. Nature herself seemed to support these ideas. When contemplating the stars, it struck me powerfully that I could not make out a star with nearly as much clarity when I stared at it with intense, direct and unwavering focus, as when I allowed my eye to glance only in the area around it. I was not, naturally, aware at that time that this seeming contradiction was caused by the center of the visual field being less sensitive to weak light than the outer parts of the retina. This understanding, along with other knowledge, came later during an eventful five-year period, during which I abandoned the prejudices of my former lowly position in life and forgot about being a bellows-mender through very different pursuits. But at the time I'm describing, the parallel that a casual observation of a star provided to the conclusions I had already reached struck me with the power of definite proof, and I then finally decided on the path I would later follow.

It was late when I got home, and I went straight to bed. My mind was too busy to sleep, though, and I spent the entire night lost in thought. I got up early the next morning and managed once again to avoid my creditors, then hurried eagerly to the bookseller's stall. I spent what little cash I had on some books about mechanics and practical astronomy. After getting home safely with these books, I dedicated every free moment to reading them, and soon made enough progress in these subjects that I felt ready to carry out my plan. During this time, I also did everything I could to win over the three creditors who had been causing me so much trouble. I eventually succeeded in this—partly by selling enough of my household furniture to pay off half of what I owed them, and partly by promising to pay the rest once I completed a small project I told them I was working on, and for which I asked for their help. Through these methods— since they were simple men—I had little trouble getting them to support my goal.

"With everything arranged this way, I managed, with my wife's help and using the utmost secrecy and caution, to sell off what property I had left, and to borrow small amounts of money under various excuses, without worrying about how I would pay it back later, accumulating a considerable sum of ready cash. Using these funds, I gradually purchased very fine cambric muslin in twelve-yard pieces, twine, a supply of rubber varnish, a large and deep wicker basket made to my specifications, and several other items needed to build and equip a balloon of extraordinary size. I instructed my wife to sew this together as quickly as possible and gave her all the necessary details about the specific method to follow. Meanwhile, I worked the twine into a net of sufficient size, fitted it with a hoop and the required cords, bought a quadrant, a compass, a telescope, a standard barometer with some important modifications, and two astronomical instruments that aren't widely known. I then found opportunities to transport by night to a secluded location east of Rotterdam five iron-reinforced barrels that could hold about fifty gallons each and one larger barrel, six tin tubes three inches in diameter with the proper shape and ten feet in length, a quantity of a particular metallic substance or semi-metal that I won't name, and a dozen glass bottles of a very common acid. The gas that would be produced from these materials is a gas that has never been created by anyone other than myself—or at least never used for any similar purpose. I would have no problem revealing this secret, except that it rightfully belongs to a citizen of Nantes, France, who shared it with me under certain conditions. This same person showed me, without knowing my intentions at all, a method for making balloons from the membrane of a certain animal, through which almost no gas could escape. However, I found this approach far too expensive and wasn't certain overall whether cambric muslin with a coating of rubber gum wouldn't work just as well. I mention this detail because I think it's likely that this person may later attempt a balloon ascent using the novel gas and material I've described, and I don't want to rob him of the credit for a very remarkable invention."

At the exact location where I planned to position each of the smaller barrels during the balloon's inflation, I secretly dug a hole two feet deep; these holes created a circle twenty-five feet across. At the center of this circle, which was the designated spot for the large barrel, I also dug a hole three feet deep. In each of the five smaller holes, I placed a container holding fifty pounds, and in the larger one I put a keg containing one hundred and fifty pounds of gunpowder. I properly connected these containers and the keg with covered fuses; after inserting about four feet of slow-burning fuse into one of the containers, I filled in the hole and positioned the barrel over it, leaving the other end of the fuse sticking out about an inch and barely visible beyond the barrel. I then filled in the remaining holes and placed the barrels over them in their intended positions.

Besides the items listed above, I transported to the storage facility and hid there one of M. Grimm's enhanced versions of the device for compressing atmospheric air. However, I discovered this machine needed significant modifications before it could be suitable for my intended use. Through intense work and constant determination, I eventually achieved complete success in all my preparations. My balloon was finished quickly. It could hold more than forty thousand cubic feet of gas and would lift me easily, I estimated, along with all my equipment, and if I handled everything correctly, with one hundred and seventy-five pounds of ballast as well. It had been given three layers of varnish, and I found the cotton muslin worked perfectly as a substitute for silk, being just as durable and considerably more affordable.

Everything was now ready, so I made my wife swear an oath of secrecy about all my actions from the day I first visited the bookseller's stall. I promised her that I would return as soon as circumstances allowed, gave her what little money I had remaining, and said farewell. I truly had no concerns about her well-being. She was what people call a capable woman and could handle worldly matters without my help. To be honest, I believe she always viewed me as a lazy boy, a mere burden, good for nothing except daydreaming, and she was probably relieved to see me go. It was a dark night when I said goodbye to her, and taking with me, as my assistants, the three creditors who had caused me so much trouble, we carried the balloon, along with the basket and equipment, by an indirect route, to the location where the other items were stored. We found everything there undisturbed, and I immediately got down to business.

"It was April first. The night, as I mentioned earlier, was dark; not a single star could be seen; and a light rain, falling on and off, made us extremely uncomfortable. But my main worry was about the balloon, which, despite the protective coating it had, was starting to become quite heavy from the moisture; the powder was also at risk of being damaged. So I kept my three assistants working very hard, packing ice around the central barrel and mixing the acid in the other containers. However, they wouldn't stop pestering me with questions about what I planned to do with all this equipment, and they expressed great unhappiness about the awful work I was making them do. They couldn't understand, they said, what good could possibly come from getting soaked to the bone just to participate in such terrible rituals. I started to feel worried and worked as hard as I could, because I truly believed these fools thought I had made a deal with the devil, and that what I was doing now was nothing short of evil. I was therefore very afraid they might abandon me completely. I managed, however, to calm them down by promising to pay all their debts in full as soon as I could finish the current task. They naturally put their own spin on these words, imagining, no doubt, that I would somehow get my hands on enormous amounts of cash; and as long as I paid them everything I owed, plus a little extra for their trouble, I'm sure they didn't care much what happened to either my soul or my body."

In roughly four and a half hours, I discovered the balloon had inflated enough. I then attached the basket and placed all my equipment inside it—making sure not to forget the condensing device, a generous supply of water, and a substantial amount of food, including pemmican, which packs considerable nutrition into a relatively small space. I also placed a pair of pigeons and a cat in the basket. Dawn was approaching, and I felt it was the right time to leave. I dropped a lit cigar on the ground, making it appear accidental, and used the opportunity of bending down to retrieve it to secretly light the piece of slow-burning fuse, whose tip, as I mentioned earlier, extended just slightly beyond the bottom edge of one of the smaller barrels. This action went completely unnoticed by the three creditors; and, leaping into the basket, I immediately severed the single rope that anchored me to the ground, and was delighted to discover that I rose upward, effortlessly carrying one hundred and seventy-five pounds of lead ballast, with the capacity to have lifted just as much more.

I had barely reached a height of fifty yards when a terrifying hurricane of fire, smoke, and sulfur came roaring and rumbling up after me in the most horrible and chaotic way. The violent blast carried with it legs and arms, gravel, burning wood, and blazing metal so dense that my heart sank within me, and I collapsed in the bottom of the basket, shaking with complete terror. I now realized that I had completely miscalculated the situation, and that the main effects of the explosion were still to come. Within less than a second, I felt all the blood in my body rushing to my head, and immediately after, a shock that I will never forget burst suddenly through the night and seemed to tear the very sky apart. When I later had time to think about it, I understood that the extreme violence of the explosion, as it affected me, was due to my position directly above it, right in the path of its greatest force. But at that moment, I could only think about staying alive. The balloon first deflated, then violently inflated, then spun around and around with terrible speed, and finally, swaying and lurching like a drunk person, threw me with tremendous force over the edge of the basket, leaving me hanging at a frightening height with my head pointing down and my face turned outward, suspended by a thin rope about three feet long that had accidentally fallen through a crack near the bottom of the wicker basket, and in which my left foot had fortunately become tangled as I fell. It is impossible—completely impossible—to properly imagine the horror of my situation. I gasped desperately for air—a trembling like a fever shook every nerve and muscle in my body—I felt my eyes bulging from their sockets—a terrible nausea overcame me—and finally I lost consciousness.

I can't say how long I stayed in that condition. It must have been quite a while though, because when I started to regain consciousness, I saw daybreak approaching, the balloon floating at an enormous height above an endless ocean, with no sign of land visible anywhere within the vast horizon. My feelings upon recovering, however, weren't nearly as agonizing as you might expect. In fact, there was something almost insanely calm about the way I began to assess my situation. I lifted each of my hands to my eyes, one at a time, and wondered what could have caused my veins to swell and my fingernails to turn such a horrible black color. I then carefully examined my head, shaking it several times and feeling it with careful attention, until I convinced myself that it wasn't, as I had more than half suspected, larger than my balloon. Then, acting like I knew what I was doing, I felt around in both my trouser pockets, and when I discovered that my writing tablets and toothpick case were missing, I tried to figure out what had happened to them. When I couldn't, I felt incredibly frustrated. It then dawned on me that my left ankle joint was causing me great discomfort, and a vague awareness of my situation started to creep into my mind. But strangely enough, I felt neither amazed nor terrified. If I experienced any emotion at all, it was a kind of amused satisfaction with the cleverness I was about to demonstrate in getting myself out of this predicament. I never once doubted that I would ultimately be safe. For several minutes I remained lost in deep thought. I clearly remember repeatedly pressing my lips together, placing my index finger alongside my nose, and making other gestures and facial expressions typical of people who, comfortable in their armchairs, contemplate complex or important matters. Having gathered my thoughts sufficiently, as I believed, I now very carefully and deliberately reached behind my back and unfastened the large iron buckle that belonged to the waistband of my trousers. This buckle had three prongs that were somewhat rusty and turned with great difficulty on their pivot. After some effort, I managed to position them at right angles to the main body of the buckle, and I was pleased to find they stayed firmly in that position. Gripping this makeshift tool between my teeth, I began to untie the knot of my necktie. I had to pause several times before I could complete this maneuver, but I eventually succeeded. I then secured the buckle to one end of the necktie, and tied the other end tightly around my wrist for extra security. Drawing my body upward with tremendous muscular effort, I managed on my very first attempt to throw the buckle over the edge of the basket, where it caught in the circular rim of the wickerwork just as I had hoped.

My body was now leaning toward the side of the basket at roughly a forty-five-degree angle, but this doesn't mean I was only forty-five degrees below vertical. Far from it—I still lay nearly parallel to the horizon because my changed position had pushed the bottom of the basket considerably outward from where I hung, putting me in the most dangerous and deadly situation imaginable. It's important to remember, though, that when I first fell from the basket, if I had fallen with my face toward the balloon instead of away from it as actually happened, or if the rope suspending me had hung over the upper edge instead of through a crack near the bottom of the basket—it's easy to see that in either of these scenarios, I wouldn't have been able to accomplish even what I had managed so far, and the remarkable adventures of Hans Pfaall would have been completely lost to future generations. I had every reason to feel thankful, therefore, although in reality I was still too dazed to feel anything at all, and I hung there for perhaps fifteen minutes in that bizarre position without making the slightest additional effort, in a strangely peaceful state of mindless contentment. But this sensation quickly faded away, replaced by terror, panic, and a bone-chilling sense of complete helplessness and doom. The truth was that the blood that had been building up so long in the vessels of my head and throat, which had previously lifted my spirits with madness and delirium, had now started flowing back to where it belonged, and the clarity this brought to my understanding of the danger only served to strip away my composure and courage to face it. Fortunately for me, this weakness didn't last very long. Just in time, the spirit of desperation came to my aid, and with wild screams and thrashing movements, I hauled my entire body upward until finally, gripping the longed-for rim with a grip like a vise, I twisted myself over it and tumbled headfirst and trembling into the basket.

It wasn't until some time later that I regained my composure enough to focus on the routine maintenance of the balloon. When I finally did examine it carefully, I discovered to my immense relief that it remained undamaged. All my equipment was intact, and fortunately, I hadn't lost any ballast or supplies. In fact, I had secured everything so thoroughly in their positions that such a mishap was completely impossible. When I checked my watch, it showed six o'clock. I was still climbing rapidly, and my barometer indicated a current altitude of three and three-quarter miles. Directly below me in the ocean lay a small dark object, somewhat elongated in form, appearing roughly the size of, and bearing a striking resemblance to, one of those children's toys known as a domino. When I focused my telescope on it, I could clearly make out that it was a British ninety-four-gun warship, sailing close to the wind and rolling heavily in the waves with its bow pointed toward the west-southwest. Apart from this vessel, I could see nothing except the ocean and the sky, along with the sun, which had risen long ago.

"It is now high time that I should explain to your Excellencies the purpose of my dangerous journey. Your Excellencies will remember that desperate circumstances in Rotterdam had finally driven me to the decision of taking my own life. It was not, however, that I had any real hatred for life itself, but that I was tormented beyond what I could bear by the additional miseries that came with my situation. In this frame of mind, wanting to live, yet tired of living, the book at the bookseller's stall opened up a possibility to my imagination. I then finally made up my mind. I decided to leave, yet live—to abandon the world, yet continue to exist—in short, to stop speaking in riddles, I resolved, whatever might happen, to force my way, if I could, to the moon. Now, so that I should not be thought more of a madman than I actually am, I will describe, as well as I am able, the reasoning which led me to believe that an accomplishment of this kind, although without doubt difficult, and undeniably full of danger, was not absolutely, to a bold spirit, beyond the boundaries of the possible."

"The moon's actual distance from the earth was the first thing to be attended to. Now, the mean or average interval between the centers of the two planets is 59.9643 of the earth's equatorial radii, or only about 237,000 miles. I say the mean or average interval, but it must be kept in mind that the form of the moon's orbit being an ellipse of eccentricity amounting to no less than 0.05484 of the major semi-axis of the ellipse itself, and the earth's center being situated in its focus, if I could, in any manner, manage to meet the moon, as it were, in its perigee, the above mentioned distance would be significantly reduced. But, to say nothing at present of this possibility, it was very certain that, at all events, from the 237,000 miles I would have to subtract the radius of the earth, say 4,000, and the radius of the moon, say 1,080, in all 5,080, leaving an actual interval to be crossed, under average circumstances, of 231,920 miles. Now this, I considered, was no very extraordinary distance. Traveling on land has been repeatedly accomplished at the rate of thirty miles per hour, and indeed a much greater speed may be expected. But even at this velocity, it would take me no more than 322 days to reach the surface of the moon. There were, however, many details leading me to believe that my average rate of traveling might possibly very much exceed that of thirty miles per hour, and, as these considerations did not fail to make a deep impression upon my mind, I will mention them more fully hereafter."

The next point to be considered was a matter of far greater importance. From readings provided by the barometer, we discover that when ascending from the earth's surface, at a height of 1,000 feet, we have left below us about one-thirtieth of the entire mass of atmospheric air; at 10,600 feet we have climbed through nearly one-third; and at 18,000 feet, which is close to the elevation of Cotopaxi, we have overcome one-half the material, or at least one-half the weighable mass of air surrounding our planet. It is also calculated that at an altitude not exceeding one-hundredth of the earth's diameter—that is, not exceeding eighty miles—the thinning of air would be so extreme that animal life could not possibly be sustained, and furthermore, that the most sensitive instruments we have for detecting the presence of the atmosphere would be insufficient to confirm its existence. But I did not fail to notice that these latter calculations are based entirely on our experimental knowledge of air's properties and the mechanical laws governing its expansion and compression in what may be called, relatively speaking, the immediate vicinity of the earth itself; and at the same time, it is assumed that animal life is and must be fundamentally incapable of adaptation at any given unreachable distance from the surface. Now, all such reasoning based on such data must, naturally, be simply analogical. The greatest height ever reached by man was 25,000 feet, achieved in the aeronautic expedition of Messieurs Gay-Lussac and Biot. This is a modest altitude, even when compared with the eighty miles in question; and I could not help thinking that the subject allowed room for doubt and great scope for speculation.

"But in reality, when ascending to any particular height, the measurable amount of air overcome during any further climb is not at all proportional to the extra altitude gained (as can be clearly understood from what has been explained earlier), but rather follows a constantly diminishing ratio. It is therefore clear that, no matter how high we climb, we cannot, in the literal sense, reach a boundary beyond which no atmosphere exists. It must be present, I reasoned; even though it may be present in a state of endless thinning."

"On the other hand, I was aware that arguments have not been lacking to prove the existence of a real and definite limit to the atmosphere, beyond which there is absolutely no air whatsoever. But a circumstance which has been overlooked by those who argue for such a limit seemed to me, although no positive refutation of their belief, still a point worthy of very serious investigation. When comparing the intervals between the successive arrivals of Encke's comet at its perihelion, after accounting, in the most exact manner, for all the disturbances due to the attractions of the planets, it appears that the periods are gradually diminishing;

that is to say, the major axis of the comet's ellipse is growing shorter, in a slow but perfectly regular decrease. Now, this is precisely what ought to be the case, if we suppose a resistance experienced by the comet from an extremely rare ethereal medium pervading the regions of its orbit. For it is evident that such a medium must, in retarding the comet's velocity, increase its centripetal force by weakening its centrifugal force. In other words, the sun's attraction would be constantly gaining greater power, and the comet would be drawn nearer at every revolution. Indeed, there is no other way of accounting for the variation in question. But again: The real diameter of the same comet's nebulosity is observed to contract rapidly as it approaches the sun, and dilate with equal rapidity in its departure towards its aphelion. Was I not justified in supposing with M. Valz, that this apparent condensation of volume has its origin in the compression of the same ethereal medium I have spoken of before, and which is only denser in proportion to its solar vicinity? The lenticular-shaped phenomenon, also called the zodiacal light, was a matter worthy of attention. This radiance, so apparent in the tropics, and which cannot be mistaken for any meteoric brightness, extends from the horizon obliquely upward, and follows generally the direction of the sun's equator. It appeared to me evidently in the nature of a rare atmosphere extending from the sun outward, beyond the orbit of Venus at least, and I believed indefinitely farther. Indeed, this medium I could not suppose confined to the path of the comet's ellipse, or to the immediate neighborhood of the sun. It was easy, on the contrary, to imagine it pervading the entire regions of our planetary system, condensed into what we call atmosphere at the planets themselves, and perhaps at some of them modified by considerations, so to speak, purely geological.

Once I embraced this perspective, I had very little doubt remaining. Assuming that during my journey I would encounter an atmosphere basically identical to what exists at Earth's surface, I believed that using M. Grimm's remarkably clever device, I could easily compress enough of it to meet my breathing needs. This would eliminate the main barrier to a trip to the moon. I had already invested considerable money and effort in modifying the device for this specific purpose, and I felt confident about its success, provided I could finish the voyage within a reasonable timeframe. This brings me back to the question of how fast such travel might be possible.

It's true that balloons, during the initial phase of their rise from the ground, are known to ascend at a relatively moderate speed. The lifting power comes entirely from the gas inside the balloon being lighter than the surrounding atmospheric air. At first glance, it doesn't seem likely that as the balloon gains height and moves through layers of atmosphere that become increasingly less dense, the original speed would increase. In other words, it doesn't appear reasonable that during this upward journey, the balloon would actually accelerate. However, I wasn't aware of any recorded balloon flight where the rate of ascent clearly decreased, though this should have happened if for no other reason than gas leaking out through poorly made balloons sealed with nothing better than ordinary varnish. It seemed, then, that the effect of such gas loss was just enough to offset the influence of some force that was causing acceleration. I began to think that if I encountered the medium I had theorized about during my journey, and if it turned out to be genuinely what we call atmospheric air, it would make relatively little difference how extremely thin I found it to be—at least regarding my ability to keep rising.

This is because the gas in my balloon would also become thinner in a similar way (and I could allow enough gas to escape to prevent the balloon from bursting), but since it would remain what it was, it would always be lighter than any mixture of nitrogen and oxygen. Meanwhile, the pull of gravity would steadily weaken in proportion to the square of the distance, and therefore, with tremendously increasing speed, I would eventually reach those far-off regions where the Earth's gravitational pull would be overcome by that of the moon. Based on this reasoning, I didn't think it was worth burdening myself with more supplies than would last for forty days.

There was still another problem that caused me some concern. It had been noted that during balloon flights to significant heights, people experience not only difficulty breathing but also severe discomfort in the head and body, often accompanied by nosebleeds and other alarming symptoms that become increasingly troublesome as altitude increases. This observation was somewhat disturbing. Wasn't it likely that these symptoms would worsen indefinitely, or at least continue until they caused death? I ultimately decided this wasn't the case. The cause could be traced to the gradual reduction of normal atmospheric pressure on the body's surface, and the resulting expansion of blood vessels near the skin—not to any actual breakdown of the body's systems, as happens with breathing difficulties, where the atmospheric density becomes chemically inadequate for proper blood renewal in the heart's chambers. Except for this lack of blood renewal, I could see no reason why life couldn't be maintained even in a complete vacuum; the expansion and contraction of the chest, commonly known as breathing, is purely a muscular action and is the cause of respiration, not its result. In other words, I believed that as the body adapted to the absence of atmospheric pressure, the painful sensations would gradually fade—and to endure them while they lasted, I counted confidently on my constitution's iron strength.

"So, if it pleases your Excellencies, I have outlined some of the reasons—though certainly not all of them—that led me to conceive the plan for a journey to the moon. I will now present to you the outcome of an endeavor that appears so bold in its conception and is, in any case, completely unprecedented in human history."

Having reached the height I mentioned earlier—three miles and three-quarters—I tossed a handful of feathers from the basket and discovered that I was still rising at a good pace; consequently, there was no need to release any ballast. This pleased me, as I wanted to keep as much weight with me as possible, for reasons I'll explain later. So far, I hadn't experienced any physical discomfort, breathing easily and feeling no headache whatsoever. The cat was resting peacefully on my jacket, which I had removed, and watching the pigeons with a casual air. The pigeons, whose legs were tied to prevent them from flying away, were busy pecking at rice grains I had scattered for them on the floor of the basket.

At twenty minutes past six o'clock, the barometer indicated an altitude of 26,400 feet, which amounts to just over five miles. The view appeared limitless. Using spherical geometry, it's quite straightforward to calculate exactly how much of the earth's surface I could see. The curved surface of any sphere segment relates to the sphere's total surface in the same way that the segment's versed sine relates to the sphere's diameter. In my situation, the versed sine— meaning the thickness of the segment below me—roughly equaled my altitude, or how high my viewing point was above the surface. 'As five miles relates to eight thousand,' would describe the proportion of earth's surface visible to me. Put simply, I could see about one sixteen-hundredth of the planet's entire surface. The ocean looked as smooth as a mirror, though when I used the telescope, I could tell it was actually quite turbulent. The ship had disappeared from view, apparently having drifted toward the east. I started experiencing sharp headaches at regular intervals, particularly around my ears—though I could still breathe reasonably well. The cat and pigeons showed no signs of discomfort at all.

At twenty minutes before seven, the balloon entered a long series of dense clouds, which caused me great trouble by damaging my condensing equipment and soaking me to the skin. This was certainly a strange encounter, since I hadn't believed it possible that clouds of this type could exist at such a high altitude. I thought it best, however, to throw out two five-pound pieces of ballast, still keeping a weight of one hundred and sixty-five pounds in reserve. After doing this, I quickly rose above the problem and immediately noticed that my rate of ascent had increased significantly. Within seconds of leaving the cloud, a flash of brilliant lightning shot from one end of it to the other, causing the entire thing to light up throughout its enormous extent, like a mass of burning and glowing charcoal. This, it's important to remember, happened in broad daylight. No imagination could picture the magnificence that might have been displayed by a similar event occurring in the darkness of night. Hell itself might have served as an appropriate comparison. Even as it was, my hair stood on end as I stared down into the gaping depths below, letting my imagination descend and wander through the strange arched chambers, crimson gulfs, and red ghostly chasms of that terrible and bottomless fire. I had truly made a narrow escape. If the balloon had stayed within the cloud just a little longer—that is to say—if the discomfort of getting wet hadn't prompted me to release the ballast, complete destruction would have been inevitable. Such dangers, though rarely considered, are perhaps the greatest risks that must be faced in balloon travel. By this time, however, I had reached too great a height to be concerned about this particular threat any longer.

"I was climbing rapidly now, and by seven o'clock the barometer showed an altitude of no less than nine and a half miles. I started having great difficulty breathing. My head was also extremely painful, and after feeling moisture on my cheeks for some time, I finally realized it was blood that was flowing quite fast from my eardrums. My eyes were also causing me great discomfort. When I passed my hand over them, they seemed to have bulged out from their sockets considerably, and all objects in the basket, and even the balloon itself, appeared warped to my sight. These symptoms were worse than I had expected and caused me some alarm. At this point, very foolishly and without thinking, I threw three five-pound pieces of ballast out of the basket. The increased rate of climb this created carried me too quickly, and without enough gradual transition, into a highly thin layer of the atmosphere, and the result nearly proved deadly to my expedition and to myself. I was suddenly struck with a convulsion that lasted for more than five minutes, and even when this somewhat stopped, I could only catch my breath at long intervals and in a gasping way—bleeding heavily all the while from my nose and ears, and even slightly from my eyes. The pigeons appeared extremely distressed and struggled to escape, while the cat cried pitifully and, with her tongue hanging from her mouth, stumbled back and forth in the basket as if poisoned. I now realized too late the great recklessness I had shown in releasing the ballast, and my anxiety was extreme. I expected nothing less than death, and death within minutes. The physical pain I endured also made me nearly unable to make any effort to save my life. I had little ability to think clearly left, and the intensity of the pain in my head seemed to be growing much worse. I realized that my senses would soon fail completely, and I had already grabbed one of the valve ropes intending to attempt a descent, when the memory of the trick I had played on the three creditors, and the possible consequences for myself if I returned, stopped me for the moment. I lay down in the bottom of the basket and tried to gather my thoughts. I succeeded enough to decide on the experiment of losing blood. Having no lancet, however, I was forced to perform the operation as best I could, and finally managed to open a vein in my right arm with the blade of my penknife. The blood had barely started flowing when I felt noticeable relief, and by the time I had lost about half a moderate basin full, most of the worst symptoms had left me entirely. I still didn't think it wise to try standing up immediately, but after tying up my arm as well as I could, I lay still for about fifteen minutes. At the end of this time I got up and found myself more free from absolute pain of any kind than I had been during the last hour and fifteen minutes of my climb. The difficulty breathing, however, was reduced only very slightly, and I realized that it would soon be absolutely necessary to use my condenser. Meanwhile, looking toward the cat, who was again comfortably settled on my coat, I discovered to my complete surprise that she had taken advantage of my illness to give birth to a litter of three little kittens. This was an addition to the number of passengers that I had not expected at all, but I was pleased by what had happened. It would give me a chance to test the truth of a theory that, more than anything else, had influenced me in attempting this climb. I had thought that the constant endurance of atmospheric pressure at the earth's surface was the cause, or nearly so, of the pain that accompanies animal life at a distance above the surface. If the kittens were found to suffer discomfort to the same degree as their mother, I would have to consider my theory wrong, but if they failed to do so, I would view it as strong confirmation of my idea."

By eight o'clock I had reached a height of seventeen miles above the earth's surface. This made it clear to me that my rate of climb was not only increasing, but that this acceleration would have been noticeable to some extent even if I hadn't released the ballast that I did. The sharp pains in my head and ears came back periodically with great intensity, and I continued to have occasional nosebleeds; but overall, I was suffering much less than I might have anticipated. However, I was finding it increasingly difficult to breathe with each passing moment, and every breath I took was accompanied by an uncomfortable spasmodic contraction of my chest. I now unpacked the condensing equipment and prepared it for immediate use.

"The view of the earth during this stage of my climb was truly beautiful. To the west, north, and south, as far as I could see, stretched an endless sheet of apparently calm ocean, which grew deeper and deeper blue with each passing moment and was already beginning to show a slight curved appearance. At an enormous distance to the east, though still clearly visible, lay the islands of Great Britain, the entire Atlantic coastlines of France and Spain, along with a small section of the northern part of Africa. Not a single building could be seen, and humanity's greatest cities had completely vanished from the earth's surface. From the Rock of Gibraltar, now reduced to a faint dot, the dark Mediterranean Sea, scattered with gleaming islands like stars across the heavens, stretched eastward as far as my eyes could reach, until its vast body of water seemed to plunge headfirst over the edge of the horizon, and I found myself straining to hear the echoes of that tremendous waterfall. Above, the sky was jet black, and the stars shone brilliantly."

Around this time, the pigeons appeared to be suffering greatly, so I decided to set them free. I first untied one of them, a beautiful gray-speckled pigeon, and placed it on the edge of the basket. The bird seemed extremely agitated, looking nervously around, flapping its wings, and making loud cooing sounds, but I couldn't convince it to leave the basket. Finally, I picked it up and threw it about six yards away from the balloon. However, instead of descending as I had expected, the pigeon struggled desperately to return, making very sharp and piercing cries. Eventually, it managed to get back to its original spot on the rim, but as soon as it did, its head dropped to its chest, and it fell dead inside the basket. The second pigeon had better luck. To prevent it from following its companion's example and trying to return, I threw it downward with all my strength, and I was relieved to see it continue falling at high speed, using its wings naturally and with ease. Within moments, it disappeared from view, and I'm confident it made it home safely. Puss, who seemed to have largely recovered from her sickness, now enjoyed a hearty meal of the dead bird before falling asleep with obvious contentment. Her kittens were quite active and showed no signs of distress whatsoever.

At eight-fifteen, when I could no longer breathe without unbearable pain, I immediately began setting up the equipment that belonged to the condenser around the basket. This equipment needs some explanation, and your Excellencies should keep in mind that my goal, first and foremost, was to completely surround myself and the cat with a barrier against the extremely thin atmosphere where I found myself, with the plan of bringing into this barrier, using my condenser, enough of this same atmosphere made dense enough for breathing. With this goal in mind, I had prepared a very strong, completely airtight, but flexible rubber bag. The entire basket was essentially placed inside this bag, which was large enough for this purpose. In other words, the bag was pulled over the whole bottom of the basket, up its sides, and then along the outside of the ropes, reaching the upper rim or hoop where the netting was connected. After pulling the bag up this way and creating a complete enclosure on all sides and at the bottom, I now needed to secure its top or opening by pulling its material over the hoop of the netting—that is, between the netting and the hoop. But if the netting were separated from the hoop to allow this to happen, what would support the basket in the meantime? The netting wasn't permanently attached to the hoop, but connected by a series of sliding loops or knots. So I only undid a few of these loops at a time, leaving the basket hanging by the rest. After inserting a section of the cloth that formed the upper part of the bag, I reattached the loops—not to the hoop, because that would have been impossible since the cloth was now in the way—but to a series of large buttons sewn to the cloth itself, about three feet below the opening of the bag, with the spaces between the buttons matching the spaces between the loops. Once this was done, I unfastened a few more loops from the rim, introduced another section of the cloth, and then connected the freed loops to their corresponding buttons. This way, I could insert the entire upper part of the bag between the netting and the hoop. It's clear that the hoop would now fall down inside the basket, while the entire weight of the basket itself, along with everything in it, would be supported only by the strength of the buttons. At first glance, this might seem like inadequate support; but it really wasn't, because the buttons were not only very strong individually, but placed so close together that only a very small portion of the total weight was carried by any single button. In fact, even if the basket and its contents had been three times heavier than they actually were, I wouldn't have worried at all. I then lifted the hoop back up inside the rubber covering and supported it at nearly its original height using three lightweight poles I had prepared for this purpose. This was done, naturally, to keep the bag stretched out at the top and to maintain the lower part of the netting in its correct position. All that remained was to seal the opening of the enclosure; and this was easily done by gathering the folds of the material together and twisting them up very tightly on the inside using a type of fixed tourniquet.

In the sides of the covering that had been fitted around the basket, three circular panes of thick but transparent glass had been installed, allowing me to see clearly in all horizontal directions around me. In the section of fabric that formed the bottom, there was also a fourth window of the same type, which lined up with a small opening in the floor of the basket itself. This allowed me to look straight down, but I had found it impossible to install any similar device overhead because of the unique way the opening there had to be sealed and the resulting wrinkles in the fabric, so I couldn't expect to see any objects directly above me. This was naturally of little importance, because even if I had been able to install a window at the top, the balloon itself would have blocked me from using it anyway.

About a foot below one of the side windows, there was a circular opening eight inches across, fitted with a brass rim that had an inner edge designed to match the threads of a screw. The large tube of the condenser was screwed into this rim, with the main body of the machine positioned inside the rubber chamber. Through this tube, a portion of the thin atmosphere surrounding us was drawn in by creating a vacuum within the machine's body, then released in a compressed state to mix with the already thin air inside the chamber. By repeating this process several times, the chamber eventually filled with air suitable for breathing. However, in such a confined space, the air would quickly become stale and unsuitable for use due to repeated contact with the lungs. The contaminated air was then expelled through a small valve at the bottom of the car—the heavy air naturally sinking into the thinner atmosphere below. To prevent creating a complete vacuum inside the chamber at any point, this air purification process was never done all at once, but carried out gradually—the valve would be opened for just a few seconds, then closed again, until one or two pumps from the condenser had replaced the expelled air. For experimental purposes, I had placed the cat and kittens in a small basket and hung it outside the car from a button near the bottom, close to the valve, so I could feed them whenever needed. I accomplished this with some risk, before sealing the chamber opening, by reaching under the car with one of the previously mentioned poles that had a hook attached to it.

By the time I had completely finished these preparations and filled the chamber as I described, it was only ten minutes before nine o'clock. Throughout the entire time I was working on this task, I suffered terrible distress from breathing difficulties, and I deeply regretted the carelessness or rather recklessness I had shown by postponing such an important matter until the last moment. But once I had finally completed it, I quickly began to experience the benefits of my invention. I could breathe freely and easily again—and really, why shouldn't I have been able to? I was also pleasantly surprised to discover that I felt significantly relieved from the intense pains that had been tormenting me up to that point. A mild headache, along with a feeling of fullness or swelling around my wrists, ankles, and throat, was almost all I had left to complain about. This made it clear that most of the discomfort caused by the removal of atmospheric pressure had actually faded away, just as I had anticipated, and that much of the pain I had endured over the past two hours should have been blamed entirely on the effects of inadequate breathing.

At twenty minutes before nine o'clock—in other words, shortly before I sealed the opening of the chamber—the mercury reached its lowest point in the barometer, which, as I previously noted, was of an extended design. At that moment it showed I had reached an altitude of 132,000 feet, or twenty-five miles, and I was therefore able to observe an area of the earth's surface equal to no less than one three-hundred-and-twentieth of its total area. By nine o'clock I had once again lost sight of land to the east, but not before I noticed that the balloon was moving quickly toward the north-northwest. The curved shape of the ocean below me was quite clear, though my view was frequently blocked by the masses of clouds that drifted back and forth. I noticed that even the thinnest vapors never rose higher than ten miles above sea level.

"At nine-thirty I conducted an experiment by tossing a handful of feathers out through the valve. They didn't float as I had anticipated; instead they plummeted straight down like a bullet, all together, at tremendous speed—disappearing from view within just a few seconds. Initially I couldn't understand this remarkable occurrence; I found it impossible to believe that my upward speed had suddenly increased so dramatically. However, it quickly dawned on me that the atmosphere had become far too thin to support even the feathers; that they were indeed falling, just as they seemed to be, at great speed; and that I had been caught off guard by the combined velocities of their downward motion and my own upward movement."

By ten o'clock I discovered that I had very little to demand my immediate attention. Everything was running smoothly, and I believed the balloon was rising with a speed that was constantly increasing, though I no longer had any way to measure how much the speed was growing. I felt no pain or discomfort of any kind, and my spirits were better than they had been at any time since leaving Rotterdam. I kept myself busy by checking the condition of my various equipment, and then by refreshing the air inside the chamber. I decided to take care of this latter task at regular forty-minute intervals, more for the sake of maintaining my health than because such frequent air renewal was absolutely essential. Meanwhile, I couldn't help but let my mind wander. My imagination ran wild in the strange and dreamlike regions of the moon. My mind, feeling free for once, wandered freely among the constantly changing marvels of a mysterious and shifting landscape. Sometimes there were ancient and weathered forests, steep cliffs, and waterfalls crashing loudly into bottomless chasms. Then I would suddenly find myself in quiet midday solitudes, where no earthly wind ever entered, and where vast fields of poppies and delicate, lily-like flowers stretched endlessly into the distance, all silent and still forever. Then again I traveled far down into another realm where everything was one dim and hazy lake, bordered by clouds. And from this sorrowful water rose a forest of tall exotic trees, like a wilderness made of dreams. And I remember that the shadows of the trees that fell upon the lake didn't remain on the surface where they landed, but sank slowly and steadily down, mixing with the waves, while from the tree trunks other shadows kept emerging, taking the place of their buried companions. "This then," I said thoughtfully, "is exactly why the waters of this lake grow darker with age, and more sorrowful as time passes." But fantasies like these weren't the only things occupying my mind. Terrors of the most harsh and frightening nature would too often force themselves into my thoughts, and shake the very core of my soul with just the possibility that they might be real. Yet I wouldn't allow my thoughts to focus on these darker imaginings for any extended time, correctly reasoning that the real and tangible dangers of the journey were enough to require my complete attention.

At five o'clock in the evening, while I was working to refresh the air inside the chamber, I took the chance to observe the cat and her kittens through the valve. The mother cat seemed to be suffering greatly once again, and I felt certain that her distress was mainly due to breathing difficulties. However, my experiment with the kittens had produced very unusual results. I had naturally expected to see them show signs of pain, though perhaps less severe than their mother's, and this would have been enough to support my theory about the normal tolerance of atmospheric pressure. But I wasn't prepared to discover, upon careful examination, that they were clearly in excellent health, breathing easily and steadily, and showing absolutely no signs of discomfort whatsoever. I could only explain this by expanding my theory and considering that the extremely thin atmosphere around us might not be, as I had assumed, chemically inadequate to sustain life, and that someone born in such conditions might possibly be unaware of any problems with breathing it, while being moved to the thicker air layers near the earth might cause suffering similar to what I had recently experienced. It has been a source of deep regret ever since that a clumsy accident at this moment caused me to lose my small family of cats and robbed me of the understanding that continued experimentation might have provided. While reaching my hand through the valve with a cup of water for the old cat, my shirt sleeves got caught in the loop that held the basket, and in an instant, pulled it loose from the bottom. Even if the whole thing had literally vanished into thin air, it couldn't have disappeared from my view more suddenly and immediately. Without question, less than a tenth of a second passed between the basket breaking free and its complete and total disappearance along with everything inside it. I sent my best wishes with it toward the earth, but naturally, I held no hope that either the cat or her kittens would survive to tell the story of their accident.

"At six o'clock, I noticed a large portion of the earth's visible surface to the east covered in thick shadow, which kept advancing rapidly until, at five minutes before seven, the entire landscape in view was wrapped in the darkness of night. However, it wasn't until much later that the rays of the setting sun stopped illuminating the balloon, and this situation, though completely expected, still gave me tremendous pleasure. It was clear that in the morning, I would see the rising sun many hours before the citizens of Rotterdam would, despite their location being much farther east, and thus, day after day, depending on how high I climbed, I would enjoy sunlight for increasingly longer periods. I decided then to keep a journal of my journey, counting the days as continuous twenty-four-hour periods, without considering the intervals of darkness."

At ten o'clock, feeling drowsy, I decided to lie down for the rest of the night; but here a problem arose, which, obvious as it might seem, had escaped my notice until the very moment I'm describing. If I fell asleep as I planned, how would the air in the chamber be refreshed during that time? To breathe it for more than an hour at most would be impossible, or even if this period could be stretched to an hour and fifteen minutes, the most devastating consequences might follow. Thinking about this dilemma caused me considerable anxiety; and it will hardly be believed that, after the dangers I had faced, I should view this matter so seriously as to abandon all hope of achieving my ultimate goal, and finally resign myself to the necessity of descending. But this hesitation lasted only briefly. I realized that man is utterly enslaved by habit, and that many aspects of his daily routine are considered absolutely essential, which are only so because he has made them customary. It was absolutely certain that I could not go without sleep; but I could easily train myself to feel no discomfort from being woken at hourly intervals throughout my entire rest period. It would take no more than five minutes to completely refresh the atmosphere, and the only real challenge was to devise a way of waking myself at the right moment to do so. But this was a problem which, I'm willing to admit, caused me considerable difficulty to solve. Certainly, I had heard of the student who, to prevent himself from falling asleep over his books, held in one hand a copper ball, whose loud crash into a basin of the same metal on the floor beside his chair effectively startled him awake whenever drowsiness overcame him. My situation, however, was entirely different, and offered no opportunity for any similar approach; for I didn't want to stay awake, but to be awakened from sleep at regular time intervals. I finally came up with the following solution, which, simple as it may appear, was welcomed by me at the moment of its discovery as an invention fully equal to that of the telescope, the steam engine, or the art of printing itself.

"It's important to note that the balloon, at the height it had now reached, kept moving upward with a steady and unwavering climb, and the basket followed with such perfect stability that it would have been impossible to detect even the slightest movement or shaking. This situation greatly helped me with the plan I now decided to put into action. My water supply had been loaded onto the balloon in barrels that each held five gallons, and they were arranged very securely around the inside of the basket. I loosened one of these barrels, and taking two ropes, I tied them tightly across the rim of the wicker basket from one side to the other, placing them about a foot apart and parallel to each other so they formed a kind of platform on which I placed the barrel, securing it in a horizontal position. About eight inches directly below these ropes, and four feet from the bottom of the basket, I attached another shelf—but this one was made of thin wood planking, being the only similar piece of wood I had available. On this lower shelf, and positioned exactly beneath one of the edges of the barrel, I placed a small clay pitcher. I then drilled a hole in the end of the barrel above the pitcher, and fitted it with a plug made of soft wood, carved in a tapering or cone-like shape. I pushed this plug in or pulled it out, as needed, until, after several attempts, it reached exactly the right tightness so that the water, seeping from the hole and dropping into the pitcher below, would fill the pitcher completely in exactly sixty minutes. This was, naturally, something that could be quickly and easily determined by observing how much of the pitcher filled up in any specific amount of time. Having set all this up, the rest of my plan becomes clear. My bed was arranged on the floor of the basket so that when I lay down, my head would be positioned directly below the opening of the pitcher. It was obvious that after an hour had passed, the pitcher, becoming full, would be forced to overflow, and it would overflow at the opening, which sat slightly lower than the edge. It was also clear that the water falling from a height of more than four feet could only fall onto my face, and the certain result would be to wake me up immediately, even from the deepest sleep possible."

It was completely eleven o'clock by the time I had finished these preparations, and I immediately went to bed, fully confident in how well my invention would work. I wasn't let down in this regard. Exactly every sixty minutes, my reliable timepiece woke me up, and after emptying the pitcher into the opening of the barrel and taking care of the condenser duties, I went back to bed. These regular breaks in my sleep bothered me even less than I had expected; and when I finally got up for the day, it was seven o'clock, and the sun had risen many degrees above my horizon line.

April 3rd. I discovered the balloon at an enormous height, and the earth's visible curvature had increased significantly. Beneath me in the ocean lay a group of black dots, which were certainly islands. In the distance to the north, I noticed a thin, white, and extremely bright line or streak along the horizon's edge, and I felt confident in assuming it was the southern edge of the Polar Sea ice. My curiosity was tremendously aroused, as I hoped to travel much further north and might eventually find myself positioned directly over the Pole itself. I now regretted that my great altitude would, in such a case, prevent me from conducting as precise an examination as I desired. Nevertheless, much could still be determined. Nothing else extraordinary happened during the day. All my equipment continued functioning properly, and the balloon kept rising without any noticeable swaying. The cold was severe and forced me to bundle up tightly in an overcoat. When darkness fell over the earth, I went to bed, even though bright daylight surrounded my immediate location for many hours afterward. The water-clock performed its function reliably, and I slept soundly until the following morning, except for the regular interruption.

April 4th. I woke up feeling healthy and in good spirits, and I was amazed by the remarkable transformation that had occurred in the sea's appearance. The water had largely lost the deep blue color it had displayed up until now, becoming a grayish-white shade with a brightness that was almost blinding to look at. The islands could no longer be seen; it was impossible to determine whether they had disappeared below the horizon toward the southeast, or if my rising altitude had simply carried me beyond their view. However, I leaned toward the second explanation. The edge of ice to the north was becoming increasingly visible. The cold was not nearly as severe. Nothing significant happened, and I spent the day reading, having made sure to bring along plenty of books.

April 5th. I witnessed the remarkable sight of the sun rising while almost the entire visible surface of the earth remained shrouded in darkness. Eventually, though, the light gradually spread across everything, and I could once again see the line of ice stretching to the north. It now appeared very clear and seemed much darker than the ocean waters. I was clearly moving toward it at considerable speed. I thought I could make out a strip of land to the east, and another to the west, but I couldn't be sure. The weather remained mild. Nothing significant occurred during the day. I went to bed early.

"April 6th. I was surprised to discover the edge of ice at a fairly close distance, with a vast field of the same material extending all the way to the northern horizon. It was clear that if the balloon maintained its current path, it would soon reach the area above the Frozen Ocean, and I now felt confident that I would eventually see the Pole. Throughout the entire day I kept moving closer to the ice. As night approached, the boundaries of my horizon suddenly and significantly expanded, certainly due to the earth's shape being that of a flattened sphere, and my arrival above the compressed regions near the Arctic circle. When darkness finally came over me, I went to sleep feeling very anxious, worried that I might pass over the object of such great fascination while having no chance to observe it.

April 7th. I woke up early, and to my immense joy, I finally saw what could undoubtedly be considered the North Pole itself. It was definitely there, directly below my feet; but unfortunately, I had climbed to such an enormous height that nothing could be seen clearly. Based on the sequence of numbers showing my different altitudes at various times between six in the morning on April second and twenty minutes before nine in the morning of the same day (when the barometer stopped working), it could reasonably be concluded that the balloon had now, at four o'clock in the morning of April seventh, reached a height of certainly no less than 7,254 miles above sea level. This altitude may seem incredible, but the calculation it's based on probably produced a result much lower than the actual truth. In any case, I definitely saw the earth's complete major diameter; the entire northern hemisphere spread out below me like a flat map: and the great circle of the equator itself formed the edge of my view. Your Excellencies can easily imagine that the limited regions previously unexplored within the Arctic circle, though located directly beneath me and therefore visible without appearing compressed, were still relatively too small and too far from my viewing point to allow for detailed examination. However, what I could observe was remarkable and thrilling. North of that enormous edge I mentioned earlier, which can reasonably be called the boundary of human exploration in these areas, one continuous, or nearly continuous, sheet of ice stretched onward. In the first few degrees of this extension, its surface was noticeably flattened, then further along it became depressed into a flat plane, and finally, becoming quite concave, it ended at the Pole itself in a circular center with sharp edges, whose visible diameter created an angle of about sixty-five seconds from the balloon's position, and whose dark color, changing in depth, was always darker than any other spot on the visible hemisphere, and sometimes deepened into complete and impenetrable blackness. Beyond this, little more could be determined. By noon the circular center had significantly shrunk in size, and by seven in the evening I lost sight of it completely; the balloon passed over the western edge of the ice and drifted away quickly toward the equator.

April 8th. I noticed a significant decrease in the earth's apparent size, along with a substantial change in its overall color and appearance. The entire visible area displayed varying degrees of a pale yellow tint, and some sections had developed a brightness that was almost painful to look at. My downward view was also considerably blocked by the thick atmosphere near the surface, which was heavy with clouds. Between these cloud masses, I could only occasionally catch a glimpse of the earth itself. This problem with direct vision had been bothering me more or less for the past forty-eight hours, but my current tremendous height seemed to push the floating vapor masses closer together, making the inconvenience increasingly obvious as I climbed higher. Even so, I could easily tell that the balloon was now floating above the Great Lakes region of North America and was traveling due south, which would take me toward the tropics. This situation filled me with deep satisfaction, and I welcomed it as a promising sign of eventual success. In fact, the direction I had been following up to this point had made me anxious, because it was clear that if I had continued on that path much longer, there would have been no chance of reaching the moon at all, since its orbit is tilted to the ecliptic at only the small angle of 5° 8′ 48″.

April 9th. Today the earth's diameter appeared much smaller, and the surface color grew deeper yellow with each passing hour. The balloon maintained its steady southern course and reached the northern edge of the Gulf of Mexico at nine P.M.

April 10th. I was suddenly awakened from sleep around five o'clock this morning by a loud, crackling, and terrifying sound that I couldn't explain in any way. The sound lasted only briefly, but while it continued, it was unlike anything I had ever heard before. Naturally, I became extremely alarmed, initially thinking the noise came from the balloon bursting. However, I carefully examined all my equipment and found nothing wrong. I spent most of the day thinking about this extraordinary event, but I couldn't find any way to explain what had happened. I went to bed feeling unsatisfied and filled with great worry and unease.

"April 11th. I discovered a shocking decrease in the earth's visible size, and a significant increase, now noticeable for the first time, in the moon's own diameter, which was just a few days away from being full. It now demanded lengthy and exhausting work to compress enough atmospheric air within the chamber to sustain life."

April 12th. A remarkable change occurred in the balloon's direction, and though I had expected it completely, it filled me with absolute joy. After reaching approximately the twentieth parallel of southern latitude on its previous path, the balloon suddenly veered at a sharp angle toward the east, continuing this way throughout the entire day while maintaining nearly, if not exactly, the precise plane of the lunar ellipse. What deserved attention was that a very noticeable swaying in the basket resulted from this change of course—a swaying that continued, to varying degrees, for many hours.

"April 13th. I was once again deeply frightened by the return of that loud, crackling sound that had terrified me on the tenth. I spent considerable time thinking about what could be causing it, but I couldn't reach any satisfying explanation. The earth's visible size has decreased dramatically, and from the balloon it now appears to cover an angle of barely more than twenty-five degrees. The moon was completely invisible, positioned almost directly above me. I remained traveling along the same elliptical path, though I made very little eastward progress."

"April 14th. The earth's diameter is shrinking extremely rapidly. Today I became strongly convinced that the balloon was actually traveling up the line of apsides toward the point of perigee—in other words, following the direct path that would bring it straight to the moon at that part of its orbit closest to the earth. The moon itself was positioned directly overhead, and therefore hidden from my sight. Great and prolonged effort was required for the condensation of the atmosphere."

April 15th. Even the basic outlines of continents and oceans could no longer be made out on the earth's surface with any real clarity. Around noon, I became aware for the third time of that terrifying sound that had shocked me so deeply before. This time, though, it lasted for several moments and grew stronger as it went on. Finally, while I stood there stunned and filled with terror, expecting some horrible destruction I couldn't even imagine, the basket shook violently, and an enormous blazing mass of some substance I couldn't identify came roaring past the balloon with the sound of a thousand thunderclaps. After my fear and amazement had somewhat calmed down, I had little trouble assuming it must be some massive volcanic chunk thrown out from the world I was approaching so quickly, and most likely one of those unusual materials that are sometimes found on earth and called meteoric stones because we don't have a better name for them.

April 16th. Today, looking upward as best I could through each of the side windows one after the other, I saw, to my immense joy, a very small section of the moon's surface jutting out, it seemed, on all sides beyond the enormous circumference of the balloon. My excitement was overwhelming; I now had little doubt that I would soon reach the end of my dangerous journey. The work now demanded by the condenser had indeed increased to an extremely burdensome level, giving me hardly any break from effort. Sleep had become nearly impossible. I grew quite sick, and my body shook with exhaustion. It was clear that human nature could not endure this state of intense suffering much longer. During the now short period of darkness, a meteoric stone once again passed near me, and the frequency of these occurrences began to cause me great concern.

April 17th. This morning marked a turning point in my journey. It should be remembered that on the thirteenth, the earth appeared to span an angular width of twenty-five degrees. On the fourteenth, this measurement had significantly decreased; on the fifteenth, an even more striking reduction was visible; and when I went to sleep on the night of the sixteenth, I had observed an angle of no more than about seven degrees and fifteen minutes. What, then, must have been my shock upon waking from a short and restless sleep on the morning of this day, the seventeenth, to discover the surface below me so suddenly and dramatically increased in size that it now spanned no less than thirty-nine degrees in apparent angular diameter! I was stunned! No words can adequately convey the extreme, the complete horror and amazement that seized me, possessed me, and entirely overwhelmed me. My knees shook beneath me—my teeth chattered—my hair stood on end. "The balloon has actually burst!" These were the first chaotic thoughts that raced through my mind: "The balloon has definitely burst!—I was falling—falling with the most violent, the most unprecedented speed! Judging by the enormous distance already covered so quickly, it could not be more than ten minutes at most before I would hit the earth's surface and be destroyed!" But eventually, rational thought came to my rescue. I stopped; I thought carefully; and I began to have doubts. The situation was impossible. I could not reasonably have descended so rapidly. Furthermore, although I was clearly approaching the surface below me, it was at a speed nowhere near as fast as the velocity I had initially imagined with such terror. This realization helped calm my mental distress, and I eventually managed to view the phenomenon from the correct perspective. In fact, amazement must have completely clouded my judgment when I failed to notice the enormous difference in appearance between the surface below me and the surface of my home planet Earth. Earth was actually above my head, completely concealed by the balloon, while the moon—the moon itself in all its magnificence—lay beneath me, at my feet.

"The shock and amazement that filled my mind from this remarkable shift in circumstances was perhaps, when all was said and done, the most difficult part of the entire experience to understand. The dramatic change itself was not only natural and unavoidable, but had actually been expected for quite some time as something that would happen when I reached that precise point in my journey where the pull of the planet would be overcome by the pull of the satellite—or, to put it more exactly, where the gravitational force drawing the balloon toward the earth would become weaker than the gravitational force pulling it toward the moon. Certainly I woke up from a deep sleep, with all my senses scrambled, to witness a truly shocking event, and one which, though anticipated, was not anticipated at that particular moment. The rotation itself must, naturally, have occurred in a smooth and gradual way, and it is far from certain that, even if I had been awake when it happened, I would have noticed it through any physical signs of the reversal—meaning, through any discomfort or disturbance, either to my body or to my equipment."

It goes without saying that once I came to my senses about my situation and recovered from the terror that had overwhelmed every part of my mind, my attention was immediately focused entirely on studying the overall physical appearance of the moon. It spread out below me like a map—and though I estimated it was still at a considerable distance, the features of its surface appeared to my eyes with remarkably clear and completely inexplicable detail. The complete lack of any ocean or sea, and indeed of any lake or river, or any body of water at all, struck me immediately as the most extraordinary aspect of its geological makeup. Yet, strangely enough, I observed vast flat areas that were clearly formed by sediment deposits, even though most of the visible hemisphere was covered with countless volcanic mountains that were cone-shaped and looked more artificial than natural. The tallest of these mountains reached no more than three and three-quarter miles in height; but a map of the volcanic regions of the Campi Phlegraei would give your Excellencies a better understanding of their general surface than any inadequate description I might attempt to provide. Most of them were clearly erupting, and made me terrifyingly aware of their rage and power through the constant thundering of the wrongly named meteoric stones, which now shot upward past the balloon with increasingly frightening frequency.

"April 18th. Today I discovered that the moon appeared enormously larger—and the clearly increasing speed of my descent started to alarm me. It should be remembered that in the early stages of my theories about the possibility of traveling to the moon, I had heavily factored into my calculations the existence of an atmosphere near the moon that would be dense relative to the size of the planet. This was despite many opposing theories and, it should be noted, despite widespread disbelief that any lunar atmosphere existed at all. But beyond what I had already argued regarding Encke's comet and the zodiacal light, my opinion had been reinforced by certain observations made by Mr. Schroeter of Lilienthal. He observed the moon when it was two and a half days old, in the evening shortly after sunset, before the dark portion was visible, and he kept watching it until it became visible. The two crescents appeared to taper into very sharp, faint extensions, with each showing its furthest point dimly lit by the sun's rays before any part of the dark hemisphere could be seen. Shortly after, the entire dark edge became illuminated. I believed this extension of the crescents beyond the semicircle must have resulted from the bending of the sun's rays by the moon's atmosphere. I also calculated the height of the atmosphere (which could bend enough light into its dark hemisphere to create a twilight brighter than the light reflected from Earth when the moon is about 32° from new) to be 1,356 Paris feet. From this perspective, I estimated the greatest height capable of bending the solar ray to be 5,376 feet. My ideas on this subject had also been supported by a passage in the eighty-second volume of the Philosophical Transactions, which states that during an occultation of Jupiter's satellites, the third disappeared after being unclear for about 1″ or 2″ of time, and the fourth became invisible near the edge.(*4)"

I had completely relied on the resistance or, more accurately, on the support of an atmosphere that existed in the dense state I had imagined for the safety of my final descent. If I turned out to be wrong about this, I had nothing better to expect as the conclusion of my adventure than being smashed to pieces against the rough surface of the satellite. And indeed, I now had every reason to be terrified. My distance from the moon was relatively small, while the work required by the condenser hadn't decreased at all, and I could detect no sign whatsoever of the air becoming less thin.

April 19th. This morning, to my immense delight, around nine o'clock, with the moon's surface terrifyingly close and my fears at their peak, the pump of my condenser finally showed clear signs of a change in the atmosphere. By ten, I had good reason to believe its density had increased considerably. By eleven, very little effort was needed with the equipment; and at twelve o'clock, with some uncertainty, I dared to unscrew the tourniquet, when, finding no discomfort from doing so, I finally opened the rubber chamber completely and removed it from around the basket. As expected, spasms and severe headache were the immediate results of such a hasty and dangerous experiment. But these and other breathing difficulties, since they weren't severe enough to threaten my life, I decided to endure as best I could, knowing I would leave them behind as I approached the denser layers near the moon. This approach, however, remained extremely rapid; and it soon became frighteningly clear that, although I had probably been correct in expecting an atmosphere dense in proportion to the satellite's mass, I had been mistaken in assuming this density, even at the surface, would be sufficient to support the great weight contained in my balloon's basket. Yet this should have been true, and to the same degree as at Earth's surface, with the actual gravity of bodies at either planet assumed to be in proportion to the atmospheric compression. That this wasn't the case, however, my steep plunge provided ample evidence; why it wasn't so can only be explained by reference to those possible geological disturbances I mentioned earlier. In any case, I was now close to the planet, and descending with the most terrible speed. I wasted no time, therefore, in throwing overboard first my ballast, then my water containers, then my condensing equipment and rubber chamber, and finally every item within the basket. But it was all useless. I still fell with horrible speed, and was now no more than half a mile from the surface. As a final resort, therefore, having removed my coat, hat, and boots, I cut the basket itself loose from the balloon, which weighed considerably, and thus, gripping the netting with both hands, I barely had time to notice that the entire countryside, as far as I could see, was densely scattered with tiny dwellings, before I tumbled headfirst into the very center of a strange-looking city, and into the middle of a huge crowd of ugly little people, who none of them spoke a single word, or made the slightest effort to help me, but stood, like a bunch of fools, grinning ridiculously, and staring at me and my balloon sideways, with their hands on their hips. I turned away from them in disgust, and, looking up at the earth I had so recently left, and perhaps left forever, saw it like a huge, dull, copper shield, about two degrees across, fixed motionless in the sky overhead, and edged on one side with a crescent border of the most brilliant gold. No signs of land or water could be seen, and the whole thing was covered with shifting spots, and banded with tropical and equatorial zones.

"Therefore, may it please your Excellencies, after experiencing tremendous anxieties, unprecedented dangers, and unmatched escapes, I had finally, on the nineteenth day since my departure from Rotterdam, safely reached the end of what was undoubtedly the most extraordinary and momentous voyage ever completed, attempted, or imagined by any inhabitant of earth. However, my adventures still need to be told. Indeed, your Excellencies can surely understand that after living for five years on a planet that is not only deeply fascinating in its unique nature, but made even more so by its close relationship as a satellite to the world where humans live, I may possess information for the private attention of the States' College of Astronomers that is far more significant than the details, no matter how amazing, of the simple journey that ended so successfully. This is actually true. I have much—a great deal—that would bring me enormous pleasure to share. I have much to tell about the planet's climate; about its remarkable changes between hot and cold, with intense, burning sunshine for two weeks followed by more than arctic cold for the next two weeks; about the constant movement of moisture through a process like distillation in a vacuum, flowing from the area directly under the sun to the point farthest away from it; about a shifting zone of flowing water; about the people who live there; about their behaviors, traditions, and government systems; about their unusual physical structure; about their ugliness; about their lack of ears, which are useless organs in such a uniquely altered atmosphere; about their resulting lack of knowledge regarding the use and nature of speech; about what they use instead of speech through a remarkable method of communication; about the mysterious connection between each individual person on the moon and some specific individual on earth—a connection similar to and dependent on the relationship between the planet and its satellite, through which the lives and fates of the inhabitants of one world are woven together with the lives and fates of the inhabitants of the other; and most importantly, if it pleases your Excellencies—most importantly, about those dark and terrifying mysteries that exist in the outer regions of the moon—areas that, due to the almost miraculous matching of the satellite's rotation on its own axis with its orbital movement around the earth, have never been exposed, and by God's grace, will never be exposed, to examination by human telescopes. All of this, and more—much more—I would gladly describe in detail. However, to keep this brief, I must receive my reward. I am desperately longing to return to my family and my home; and as the price for any additional information from me—considering the understanding I can provide about many crucial areas of physical and metaphysical science—I must request, through the influence of your honorable organization, a pardon for the crime I committed in causing the death of my creditors when I left Rotterdam. This, then, is the purpose of this document. The person carrying it, a resident of the moon whom I have convinced and properly taught to serve as my messenger to earth, will wait for your Excellencies' decision and return to me with the requested pardon, if it can be obtained in any way."

"I have the honor to be, etc., your Excellencies' very humble servant,"

HANS PFAALL.

After finishing reading this remarkable document, Professor Rub-a-dub reportedly dropped his pipe on the ground in complete shock, while Mynheer Superbus Von Underduk removed his glasses, cleaned them, and put them in his pocket, becoming so overwhelmed that he forgot his composure and dignity entirely, spinning around three times on his heel in pure amazement and wonder. There was no question about it—the pardon would definitely be granted. At least that's what Professor Rub-a-dub declared with a strong oath, and that's what the distinguished Von Underduk ultimately believed as he took his fellow scientist's arm and, without saying anything, started heading home as quickly as possible to think about what steps they should take. When they reached the burgomaster's front door, however, the professor dared to point out that since the messenger had chosen to vanish—undoubtedly terrified by the fierce looks of Rotterdam's citizens—the pardon would be useless, since only someone from the moon would attempt such an incredibly long journey. The burgomaster agreed this observation was true, so the matter ended there. The rumors and theories, however, did not stop. Once the letter was made public, it sparked all kinds of talk and different opinions. Some people who thought they were especially clever even made fools of themselves by dismissing the entire affair as nothing more than a trick. But with these types of people, I think "trick" is just their catch-all word for anything they can't understand. As for me, I can't imagine what evidence they're basing such a claim on. Let's examine what they're saying:

First. That certain jokers in Rotterdam have particular strong dislikes toward certain mayors and astronomers.

I don't understand at all.

Secondly. A strange little dwarf and bottle conjurer, whose ears have both been cut off close to his head as punishment for some wrongdoing, has been missing for several days from the nearby city of Bruges.

Well—what of that?

Thirdly. The newspapers that were pasted all over the small balloon were Dutch newspapers, which meant they couldn't possibly have been made on the moon. These papers were filthy—extremely dirty—and Gluck, the printer, would swear on his Bible that they had been printed in Rotterdam.

He was wrong—without a doubt—completely wrong.

Fourthly, Hans Pfaall himself, that drunken scoundrel, along with the three lazy men who called themselves his creditors, were all spotted just two or three days ago in a drinking establishment on the outskirts of town, having recently come back from an overseas journey with money in their pockets.

Don't believe it—don't believe a word of it.

Finally, it's a widely held belief, or at least should be widely held, that the College of Astronomers in the city of Rotterdam, along with other colleges throughout the world—not to mention colleges and astronomers in general—are, to put it mildly, no better, no greater, and no wiser than they should be.

THE END

Thank You For Reading

You've Just Read a Piece of the Greatest Library Ever Rebuilt

Thank you for reading.

This book is one of thousands we're restoring, reimagining, and translating as part of the **Modern Library of Alexandria** — a global movement to preserve and share humanity's most important ideas.

What was once lost to fire and time is now rising again — not just as memory, but as living, breathing knowledge, freely accessible to all.

What You Can Do Next:

- **Keep Reading.**

  Discover more legendary works — in beautiful print, audiobook, or digital form — at LibraryofAlexandria.com.

- **Build Your Own Library.**

  Every title is available as a paperback, hardcover, or collectible boxset — at true printing cost. Craft a personal library worthy of display.

- **Spread the Light.**

  Share this book. Tell others about the movement. Help us translate every timeless work into every language, so no reader is ever left behind.

By finishing this book, you've already taken part in something extraordinary.

Join us at LibraryofAlexandria.com

Together, we're rebuilding the greatest library the world has ever known.

With appreciation,

The Modern Library of Alexandria Team

Visit:
www.libraryofalexandria.com
Or scan the code below:

www.ingramcontent.com/pod-product-compliance
Lightning Source LLC
Chambersburg PA
CBHW012205030726
47494CB00022B/2359